ABANDON yourself to love

by RENÉE LOCKS and JOSEPH McHugh

CELESTIAL ARTS
Millbrae, California

First printing, October 1980

Made in the
United States of America

ISBN: 0-89087-304-6
LC: 80-67343

1234567    85 84 83 82 81 80

Thank you
all
for
asking
for
seconds

Sincerely,
Joe
and
Renée

THE MIND HAS A THOUSAND EYES

THE HEART BUT ONE

Look
up
with
Joy
to the
Center

Look
up

- Ramana Maharshi

dare to be beautiful

he
who
walks
with
Beauty
has
no
need
of
fear
,
the
Sun
&
Moon
&
Stars
keep
pace
with
him

.

At any moment
I can choose the cynicism
of the known and go on,
not extending
myself
into the
unknown

Carla Needleman
a potter

the
unknown
awaits
your
kisses

joe

heaven's help
is better
than early rising

/ CERVANTES

It isn't
the thing
you do dear
dear,
It's
the thing
you
leave undone
That
gives you
a bit of a
heartache
at the
setting
Of the
Sun

Margaret E. Sangster

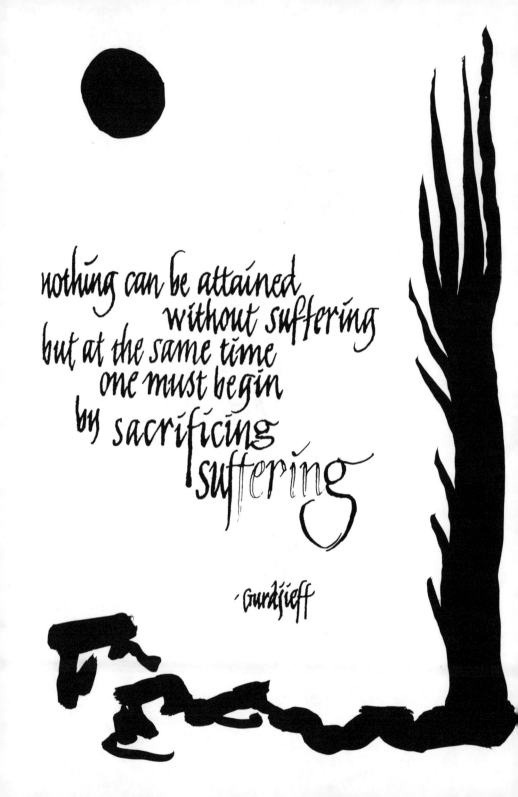

nothing can be attained
        without suffering
but at the same time
    one must begin
by sacrificing
        suffering

- Gurdjieff

I TELL YOU - THE PAST IS A PILE OF ASHES

We have
free will —
we
also
have
free
won't
•

-Renée

# Never Plays Leapfrog With Unicorns

- Old Polish Proverb

Life
is a mirror
'SMILE
at
it
.

the best way
to
rid yourself
of
troubles
is
to let them
die
of
neglect

It is a funny
thing
about life,

if you refuse
to accept
anything
but the
BEST
you
often get
it
❖

Somerset Maugham

Get up
and
out
my
friend,
the
day
is
bursting
with
moments

# O
## FRIEND,
## AWAKE & SLEEP
## NO MORE!
## THE NIGHT IS OVER
## & GONE,
## WOULD
## YOU LOSE YOUR
## DAY ALSO?

SONGS OF KABIR

*Lord, grant me pleasure daily.*

— OLD EGYPTIAN PRAYER

time time
is is
much free
better for
than the
money taking

from "A PLACE for HUMAN BEINGS"

O my soul,
do not aspire
to immortal life
but exhaust
the limits
of the possible

PINDAR
Pythian iii

If you don't know where you're going ANY ROAD WILL take you there

the Talmud

*Life is what happens to you while you are making other plans*

PLAY FOR MORE
THAN YOU CAN
AFFORD TO LOSE,
AND YOU WILL
LEARN THE GAME.

— CHURCHILL

# think

## or

# swim

*- John Stephens*

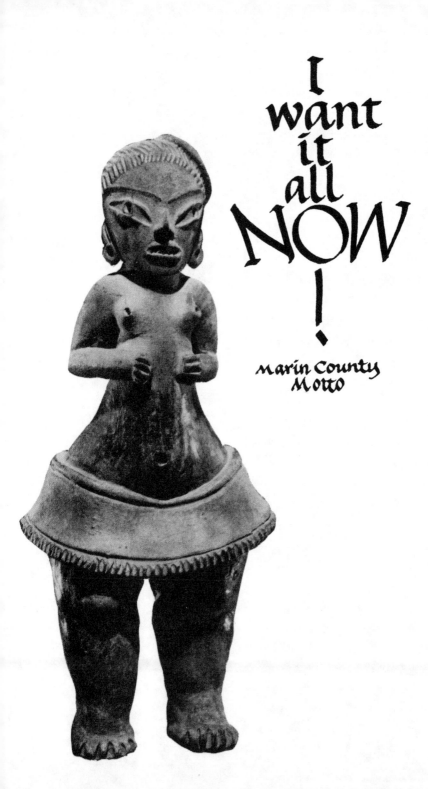

I
want
it
all
NOW
!

marin County
Motto

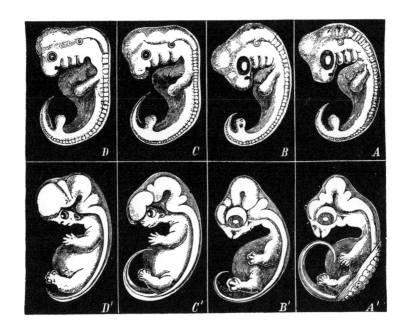

# BETTER LIVING
# THROUGH ALCHEMY

-TAO CHEMICAL CO.

# THE SOUL ATTRACTS WHAT IT LOVES & FEARS

ANDMAN KNOWS IT!
  KNOWS MOREOVER·
THAT THE WOMAN THAT GOD GAVE HIM
  MUST COMMAND
BUT MAY NOT GOVERN⁄
  SHALL ENTHRALL
BUT NOT ENSLAVE HIM·

Rudyard Kipling

Temptation
ARISES
when
a
man
is
enticed
&
lured awa

y
by
his
own
lust

james
I
:14

. a woman without a man
is like a fish
without a bicycle

Bumper Sticker

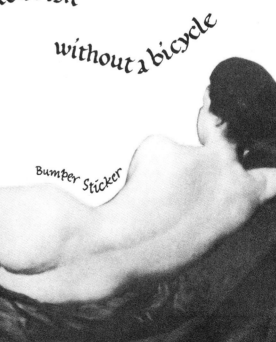

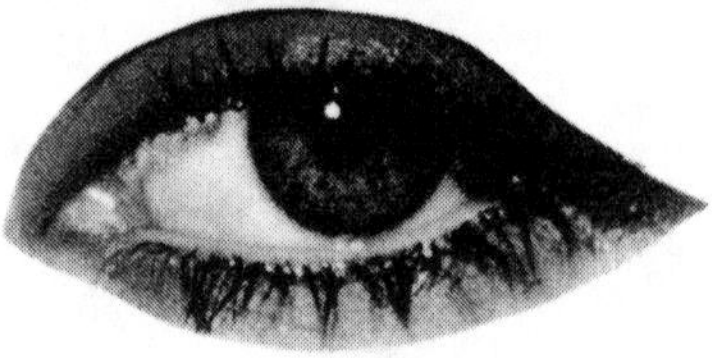

In a
woman's
eyes
deep mystery
lies
&
lies
&
lies

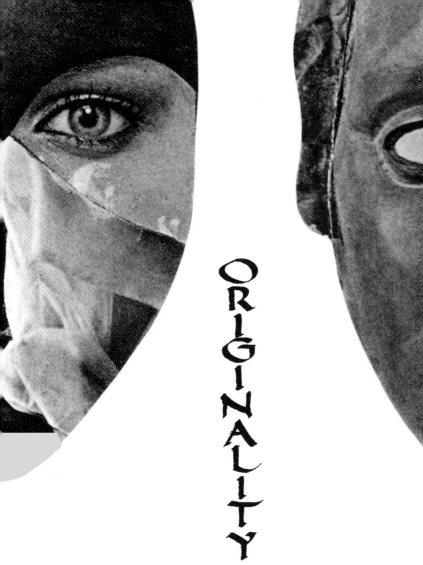

ORIGINALITY

IS SIMPLY
A FRESH PAIR of EYES

/ WOODROW WILSON

Out of a world of laughter
 Suddenly I am sad . . .
Day and night it haunts me
The kiss I never had .

    -Sydney King Russell

he left me feeling like a golden fluid pool

marva

# PLEASE
## BE PATIENT.
### GOD
## ISN'T FINISHED
## WITH ME YET.

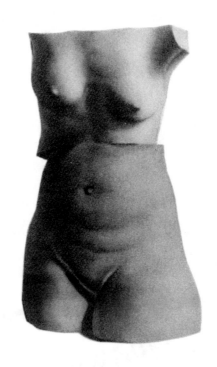

Sex without Love is an empty experience but as empty experiences go, its one of the best

WOODY ALLEN

heaven is just a sin away

-the Kendalls

Don't make the mistake of letting yesterday use up too much of today

The
mill
will
never grind
with
the
water
that
has
passed
.

Old Proverb

If the Lord wrote reports like a bureaucrat,
Moses would have suffered
a terrible hernia
lugging those tablets
down from
the mountain

Joel Ponzer

Talk not to all
of things
sublime & essential,
Seek the level of him
with whom you speak
So as not to humble
or distress him .
Be frivolous too
when you are with the frivolous,
But once in awhile, as if unsought
Or even as if thoughtlessly,
Drop into their cup,
on the form of frivolity,
A very small petal
from the flower
of your dreams
.
If it is not noticed,
recover it courteously
And always smiling, go your way.
If however, someone picks up
the frail small petal
And examines it, inhales its fragrance,
Give him forthwith,
and carefully,
a sign of discreet understanding
Then
let him behold
one of a few
of the marvelous flowers
of your garden .
Tell him of the invisible divinity
that surrounds us all
&
give him the magic word
The open sesame
to true Freedom .

THE SIGN
translated from the Spanish

YOU
HARM
A
Flower
&
YOU HAVE
HARMED
MILLIONS
OF
Stars

Under
the
cherry
blossoms
none
are
utter
strangers

-Issa

WHEN I THINK IT IS MINE
THE SNOW ON THE UMBRELLA
IS LIGHT

/KIKAKU

how beautiful it is to do nothing,
& then to rest afterward.

— SPANISH PROVERB

where
would
the
gardener
be
if
there
were
no
more
weeds

chuang Tzu

There is so much good in the worst of us,
And so much bad in the best of us,
That it ill behooves any of us
To find fault with the rest of us.

—Unknown

# SELF·ACQUAINTANCE IS A RARE CONDITION
## ~Robert Henri

If you
heard it
through the grapevine
the wine
is probably
sour

—Poor Elizabeth's Almanac

you can always get drunk from the still within

~ claude Neier

A person
has to believe
in something

·

In the meantime
I believe
I'll have
another
drink

·

W.C. Fields

# ƎXPECTATION
### is a form of
### blindness.

The most
exhausting
thing
in
life

is being
insincere

Anne Morrow Lindbergh

The True Test
of Civilization
is not the census,
nor the size of the cities,
nor the crops...

But
the kind of person
the Country
turns out.

~Emerson

YOU ARE
AMAZING
GRACE
you are a precious
JEWEL ❖ YOU ❖ ❖ ❖
SPECIAL miraculous
unrepeatable FRAGILE
FEARFUL, TENDER, lost
SPARKLING Ruby emerald
JEWEL RAINBOW SPLENDOR
P E R S O N

YOU are amazing GRACE · YOU
are a precious                    are a precious
JEWEL                              JEWEL
you, special                       you, special
miraculous                         miraculous
UNREPEATABLE                       UNREPEATABLE
FRAGILE                            FRAGILE
FEARFUL,                           FEARFUL,
TENDER,                            TENDER,
LOST SPARKLING                     LOST SPARKLING
RUBY EMERALD                       RUBY EMERALD
JEWEL                              JEWEL
RAINBOW                            RAINBOW
SPLENDOR                           SPLENDOR
PERSON                             PERSON

JOAN
BAEZ

ALL PEOPLE BRING HAPPINESS

SOME BY COMING
SOME BY GOING

From the BIG SUR INN

What is life
but a series
of inspired
follies
?
— Shaw

# make haste SLOWLY

-Ben Franklin

it is
no longer necessary
for anyone
to push the river

-a flower
doesn't speak

See the willow
by the river
there

it is

watching
the water

flow

by

*If you your lips would keep from slips,*
*Five things observe with care :*
*OF WHOM you speak, TO WHOM you speak,*
*And HOW and WHEN and WHERE.*

*–Unknown*

# Even a Lie is a psychic FACT

Jung

Love
answers
all questions
for
it ignores
questioning itself.

meher Baba

IF LOVE
IS
THE ANSWER
,
COULD YOU
PLEASEREPEAT THE
QUESTION
.

Lily Tomlin

ONE
HILL
WILL
KEEP
THE
FOOTPRINTS
OF
THE
MOON

david
morton

action

stillness

the hidden harmony
is stronger
than the visible

-HERACLITUS

CORNELL TROOPER WEBB

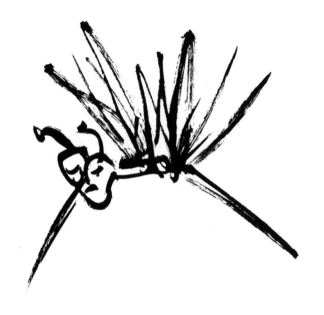

No mosquito bites from malice

-Proverb

Oh Lord,
have
mercy
&
mend
our
broken
wings

Gibran

Be like the bird, pausing in his flight
On limb too slight,
Feels it give way, yet sings,
Knowing he has wings.

—Victor Hugo

If I had my life to live over, I'd dare to make more mistakes. I'd relax, I would limber up . . .

I would take more chances... I would eat more ice cream and less beans.

You see, I'm one of those people who live sensibly and sanely hour after hour, day after day.

Oh, I've had my moments and if I had it to do over again, I'd have more of them. In fact, I'd try to have nothing else. Just moments, one after another, instead of living so many years ahead of each day.

I've been one of those persons who never goes anywhere without a thermometer, a hot water bottle, a raincoat and a parachute. If I had to do it again, I'd travel lighter.

I would start barefoot earlier in the Spring and stay that way later in the Fall. I would go to more dances. I would ride more merry-go-rounds. I would pick more daisies.

NADINE STAIR, age 85

I know I'm alright because God doesn't make screw-ups

OFF THE WALL

MOST PEOPLE
ARE JUST ABOUT
AS HAPPY AS
THEY MAKE UP
THEIR MINDS
TO BE

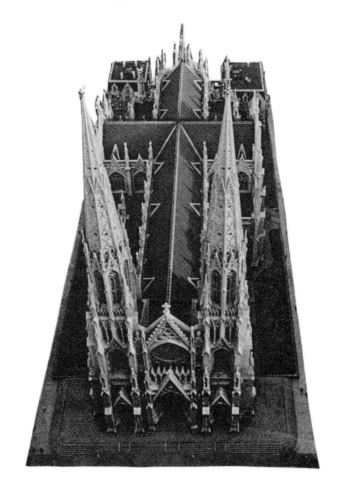

Do you know how much it co$ts
just to wake up?

-JAY STRICKLER

...what
we
need
here
is
revelation
not
revolution

~ Reverend Joel Agnew

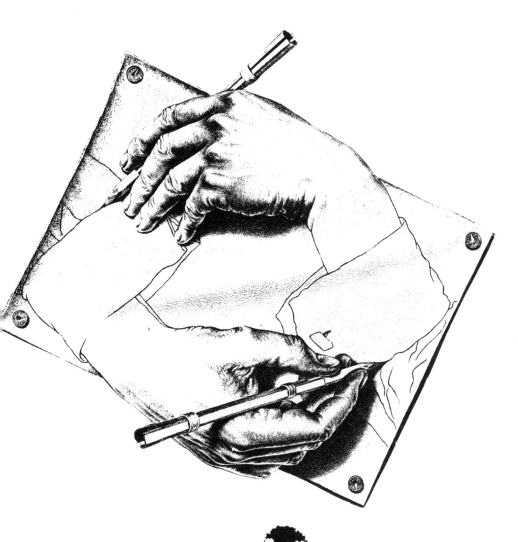

# PROCRASTINATION IS A SPONTANEOUS REORGANIZATION OF MY PRIORITIES

- MARVA

When you're
through
changing
you're
through.

Alfred P. Sloan

A GOOD
idea
can
never
drop
into
a
closed
mind

**OUT**
of
the
mouths
of
children
come

**WORDS**

we
adults
never
should
have
said

.

SHOULD

SHOULD

should

Should
Should
Should
Should
Should
Should
Should
Should
Should
Should
Should
Should
Should
Should
Should
should
Should
should
Should
should
should

SHULD!

Should

should

should

SHOULD

IT
TOOK
ME
FORTY
YEARS
ON EARTH
TO
REACH
THIS
SURE
CONCLUSION
,
THERE
IS
NO
HEAVEN
BUT
CLARITY

,

freedom
is what you do
with
what's been done
to you.

·Sartré

WE are not here TO do
what has already been DONE

-Robert Henri

We value a thing
according
to our capacity to understand it.
(If you give a diamond
to a shepherd
he will
tie it around the neck of his goat.

— Swami Tejomayanada

Too much
of
a
good thing
is
WONDERFUL

Mae West

Oh my friend
Where is Truthfulness?
        Goodness?
        Light?
The world enveils me;
  my body itself this night
  enveils my soul,
My soul like a paper lantern
  in the rainy world.

— Japanese poem

seeing
the
smile
in
your
eyes
i
have
forgotten
that
people
die

.

We bless the Lord
by dancing
DERVISH

If
I
stepped
out
of
my
body
I
would
break
into
blossoms

✳

James Wright

IT TOOK ME

Safe
upon
the
SOLID
ROCK
the ugly
HOUSES
STAND:
Come & see
my shining
PALACE
built upon
the sand.
Edna St. Vincent Millay.

We turn to God
for help
when our foundations
are shaking,
only to learn
that it is
God
who 's
shaking
them

charles c. west

life is wild

love
is
WILD
and
God
is
absolutely
WILD

-Rajneesh